Math Counts

Length

Introduction

In keeping with the major goals of the National Council of Teachers of Mathematics Curriculum and Evaluation Standards, children will become mathematical problem solvers, learn to communicate mathematically, and learn to reason mathematically by using the series Math Counts.

Pattern, Shape, and *Size* may be investigated first—in any sequence.

Sorting, Counting, and *Numbers* may be used next, followed by *Time, Length, Weight,* and *Capacity.*

Ramona G. Choos, Professor of Mathematics, Senior Adviser to the Dean of Continuing Education, Chicago State University; Sponsor for Chicago Elementary Teachers' Mathematics Club

About this Book

Mathematics is a part of a child's world. It is not only interpreting numbers or mastering tricks of addition or multiplication. Mathematics is about *ideas.* These ideas have been developed to explain particular qualities such as size, weight, and height, as well as relationships and comparisons. Yet all too often the important part that an understanding of mathematics will play in a child's development is forgotten or ignored.

Most adults can solve simple mathematical tasks without the need for counters, beads, or fingers. Young children find such abstractions almost impossible to master. They need to see, talk, touch, and experiment.

The photographs and text in these books have been chosen to encourage talk about topics that are essentially mathematical. By talking, the young reader can explore some of the central concepts that support mathematics. It is on an understanding of these concepts that a child's future mastery of mathematics will be built.

Henry Pluckrose

1995 Childrens Press® Edition
© 1994 Watts Books, London, New York, Sydney
All rights reserved.
Printed in the United States of America.
Published simultaneously in Canada.
1 2 3 4 5 6 7 8 9 0 R 04 03 02 01 00 99 98 97 96 95

Math Counts

Length

By Henry Pluckrose

Mathematics Consultant: Ramona G. Choos,
Professor of Mathematics

 CHILDRENS PRESS ®
CHICAGO

How long is the string
in this ball?

How long is this truck?
Sometimes we need
to measure things to find out
exactly how long they are.

We use the word *length*
to describe the measurement of something
from one end to the other.
We talk about the length of a swimming pool,

the length of a race,

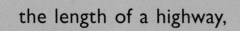
the length of a highway,

8

or a length of fabric.

You could measure the length of a table by counting in hand spans.

But people's hands are not all the same size.

You could measure the length of the lawn by counting in paces,

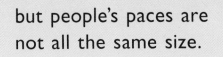
but people's paces are not all the same size.

13

If we want to measure
exactly, we have to use
a *standard measure*.
Standard measures are
the same everywhere.
A surveyor measures
the ground with a tape.
The tape is divided
into meters and centimeters
or feet and inches.

14

It is important to be able
to measure exactly.
Architects draw detailed plans
for builders to use.
They have to make sure
a building will fit on its space.

A tailor uses
exact measurements.
Short lengths are measured
in centimeters or inches.
A hundred centimeters
make one meter.
Thirty-six inches make one yard.

Scientists often study very small creatures. Tiny things are measured in millimeters. Ten millimeters make one centimeter, about one-third of an inch.

Niederhöchstadt

Frankfurt a. M. 14 km
Frankfurt a.M.

Meters and centimeters are useful
for measuring things that are not too long.
In most countries, distances between places
are measured in kilometers.
A thousand meters makes one kilometer.

A 4

Bath	4
Chippenham	17
Marlborough	35

In some countries, a different standard measure is used to show distances between places. This sign shows distances in miles. A mile is longer than a kilometer.

5 feet →

We also use meters
and centimeters,
or feet and inches,
to measure height.
The height of a person
is measured from
the soles of the feet
to the top of the head.
What is your height?

2 feet →

As you grow
you become taller.
Years ago, these
basketball players were
exactly the same height
as you are today.
How do you know?

We use the word *height*
to describe many other things.
The height of a building
is measured from the ground
to the very top.

The height of this cliff
is measured from the level
of the sea to the grassy land
at the top.

Mountains also are measured from sea level.
The peak of Mount Everest is 29,029 feet
(8,848 meters) above sea level.
Why do you think sea level is used
when giving the height of a mountain?

Aircraft pilots also measure the height that their plane is flying.

We can describe the height of things around us by comparing them with the height of our own body. These plants have not grown very tall,

but they must seem enormous
to a lizard.

27

These trees are very tall.
Their topmost branches
are far above the ground.

When trees are cut down
for timber,
the lumberjack measures
the length of each trunk,
not its height.

What is the difference between length

and height?

1995 Childrens Press® Edition
© 1994 Watts Books, London, New York, Sydney
All rights reserved.
Printed in the United States of America.
Published simultaneously in Canada.
1 2 3 4 5 6 7 8 9 0 R 04 03 02 01
00 99 98 97 96 95

Library of Congress Cataloging-in-Publication Data

Pluckrose, Henry Arthur.
    Length / Henry Pluckrose.
      p.   cm.
    Originally published: London; New York: F. Watts, 1988.
    (Math counts)
    Includes index.
    Summary: Photographs and text introduce the concept of length and how to measure it.
    ISBN 0-516-05453-8
    1. Length measurement — Juvenile literature. [1. Length measurement. 2. Measurement.]
    I. Title.
QC102.P58   1995
530.8 — dc20   94-38006
                                                                                    CIP
                                                                                    AC

Photographic credits: Chris Fairclough, 4, 5, 6, 8, 10, 11, 14, 17, 19, 23, 24, 25, 26, 28, 29;
SuperStock International, Inc., Glod Collection, 7; © Cameramann International, Ltd. 9; Unicorn
Stock Photos, © Tommy Dodson, 12, 13, © Kathryn Bellifemine, 20; PhotoEdit, © Michael
Newman, 15, 16; ZEFA, 18, 27; Photri, © Brian Drake, 21; Robert Harding Picture Library, 22;
© Sean Aidan, 30, 31

Editor: Ruth Thomson
Assistant Editor: Annabel Martin
Design: Chloë Cheesman

INDEX